The Isle of Man

A POSTCARD TOUR

VOLUME ONE – RAMSEY AND THE NORTH

compiled by

Steven Dearden and Ken Hassell

T. Kermeen of Parliament Street, Christmas Show 1907.

Richard Stenlake Publishing
1995

ISBN 1 872074 66 9

INTRODUCTION

This volume, the first of four, covers Ramsey and the north of the Isle of Man from 1900-1939, using postcards drawn from our two collections. Three future books will cover Douglas and the east; Peel and the west; and Castletown and the south.

Although the emphasis is on Ramsey here, rarer photographs of Maughold, Lezayre, Andreas, Bride, Jurby and Ballaugh have also been included, and where possible we have tried to show the people as well as the places.

Ramsey enjoys an ideal location, situated both at the mouth of the Sulby River and the foot of the wooded slopes of North Barrule. Its bay is the largest in the island, and forms a magnificent sweep of ten miles from the Point of Ayre to Maughold Head. Historically, the area has always been important, with the battle that gave the kingship of Mann to Godred Crovan fought on Sky Hill in 1079. However, despite its importance, Ramsey long remained a small settlement, and only officially became a town in 1865. Fishing and farming were the mainstays of the economy, and Ramsey acted as a port and market centre for the rich surrounding farmland.

Ramsey's growth was gradual until the arrival of the railway, and it was only upon completion of the Queen's Pier in 1884 - along with the imaginative development of the Mooragh in the 1880s – that the town blossomed into a prosperous tourist resort, second only to Douglas. Fortunately, this period of growth coincided with the development of photography and the picture postcard craze, and as a result the period has been well recorded visually.

The general history of the area has been too well covered by Constance Radcliffe to need outlining here; indeed, her books and the writings of the late Sydney Boulton have been invaluable in the preparation of our text. However, the men responsible for the invaluable pictorial record we have inherited are perhaps less well known, and a few words on the local photographers represented in this book may be in order.

From 1902 onwards, during the boom years of tourism in Ramsey and the heyday of the picture postcard, dozens of British and German publishers issued cards of the town and its better known surrounding attractions. Unfortunately, as is the case today, they tended to select the same standard views, ignoring areas not on the tourist routes. Some large publishers such as Baurs and Valentines did produce more imaginative views of a very high standard, but the widest range of subjects were photographed by Ramsey's several local photographers, who produced fine cards of the lesser known areas such as Andreas, Bride and Jurby.

G. B. Cowen, Alfred Moore, Arthur Hadley, J. Pallister and Thomas Horsfall Midwood all produced excellent photographic cards, mainly in the years up to the First World War. Only the Midwoods, a father and son team, continued to produce postcards right through to 1939, by which time they had published literally thousands of cards. There was hardly a place or event that wasn't recorded by their cameras, and they have left a priceless record of Ramsey in the earlier years of this century. Midwoods are responsible for the majority of the cards published in this book, and as their advertisements claimed, 'no collection is complete without Midwoods postcards'.

According to the town commissioners' rate list of 1880, Thomas Midwood, then aged 22, was a 'photographer, the Shore', Ramsey; a business that he probably set up when the South Promenade was constructed in 1875. Advertising in an 1889 town guide, Mr T. H. Midwood proclaimed that he had 'one of the best lighted and furnished studios in the Kingdom'.

Tom Midwood became one of Ramsey's best known townsmen and was chairman of its commissioners from 1908-1910; as well chairman of the lifeboat committee. His brother Charles ran the billiards rooms at 12 Mona Street, part of the garrison quarters that had been the home of the family for many years, while Mrs Midwood kept the boarding house 'Laureston'. After Thomas's death in 1927, the photography business was continued by his son, Charlie Midwood.

Of the other local photographers, George B. Cowen is the most notable. He studied under the early Douglas photographer Abel Lewis and became a very successful photographer and portraitist, who had formed a partnership with Alfred Moore at 23 Waterloo Road by 1889, and moved to his own premises at 56 Waterloo Road in 1894. Generally a sensitive recorder of Manx country life, his later work unfortunately tended towards fake rustic scenes recreating the atmosphere of Hall Caine's novels. Arthur Hadley came to the Isle of Man from West Bromwich, and was initially employed by Tom Midwood, although he opened his own studio near the Imperial Hotel on the South Promenade in the 1890s. As well as being a photographer, Hadley ran a billiards saloon and his later career tended more towards involvement in local politics during the early days of the labour movement. His photography business was essentially a summer one and he produced many fine studies of holiday groups at Rushen Abbey, Glen Helen, and Sulby Glen. Originally, he travelled to his locations by horse trap, but became one of the earliest users of the motor car, chauffeured around by Bobby Kneen. It was on his return from one of these trips – from Rushen Abbey in 1927 – that his car crashed at the Blackboards, and Mr Hadley suffered injuries from which he never fully recovered.

George Patterson predated the postcard era, first appearing in business near the Catholic Church in 1871, later relocating to 3 Ballure Road, and finally sharing premises in Waterloo Road with Alfred Moore around 1890.

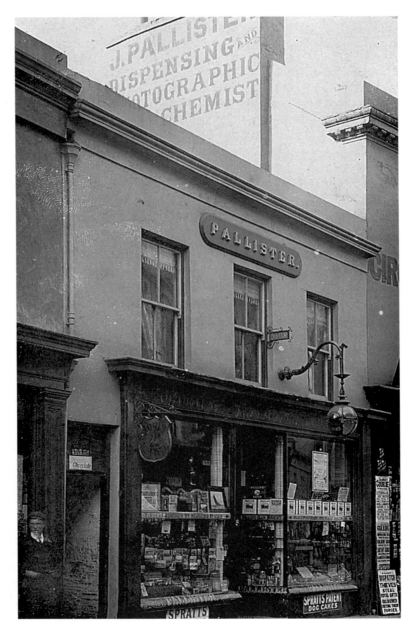

Finally, J. Pallister, a dispensing chemist, produced postcards in the early years of the century from premises at 17 Parliament Street and on the South Promenade.

We hope that the postcards of these, and the other photographers whose work appears in this book will bring back some happy memories, as well as casting light on aspects of local life that are now largely forgotten.

Steven Dearden and Ken Hassell.

Having arrived on one of the many Isle of Man Steam Packet Company vessels, the starting point for most tourists' visit to Ramsey was the Queen's Pier, photographed here by T. H. Midwood, c1905. The S.S. *Mona's Queen*, shown arriving at the pier, was built in 1885 and continued in service until 1929 by which time she was the last paddle steamer in the company fleet.

The arrival of the direct boat from Liverpool was always guaranteed to attract a crowd in pre-war days. This Midwood card shows the *Ben-My-Chree III* berthed at the 'new' landing stage, built in 1899. At Liverpool passengers would be separated into two queues, one for Ramsey, and the other for the Isle of Man! Due to the poor condition of the wooden berthing head, steamer calls ceased after Thursday 10th September 1970, when the *Manxman* called on the Belfast sailing.

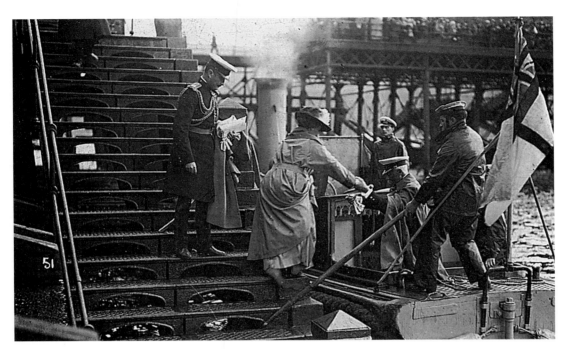

King George V helps Queen Mary into the launch to return to the Royal Yacht after their visit of July 1920. A large crowd have gathered on the pier – something unlikely to be allowed today in our security-conscious times. Sadly, the fine iron landing steps at the end of the pier have now been demolished.

The Queen's Pier, nearly half a mile in length, cost £45,000 to build and was officially opened on 22nd July, 1886. It quickly became a favourite promenading area for the town, but was also a real boost for the holiday trade in the north, with 159 landings made by passenger steamers in the first year of operation. The future of the pier today remains uncertain, but hopefully sense will prevail and ensure its preservation for the enjoyment of future generations.

This Midwood card of June 1908 shows the 6th Manchester Regiment outside the handsome red-brick shelter in Queen's Drive, on the corner of Maughold Street. Built at the turn of the century to provide a waiting room for boat passengers, a mortuary was later installed in the basement, while the main room was used as the headquarters of the Ramsey Town Band for a long time. The writer of the card says 'we didn't half wake the Ramsey folk at four in the morning!'

Volunteers prepare to march through Ramsey on the way to their camp at Milntown. The original hand-propelled Ramsey Pier passenger car can be seen on the Queen's Pier. Purchased in 1899 at the time of improvements to the pier head, it was only in 1937 that the tramway was modernised with the purchase of a Hibberd 'Planet' petrol-driven locomotive.

THE SQUARE, RAMSEY, I.O.M.

By 1934 Ramsey Market Square was often busy with charabancs. As well as other traffic, this Valentine's card shows the Fern Glen bus, a popular afternoon excursion from Ramsey at the time. Several well known businesses can also be seen – the Royal Oak Dining Rooms, Royal Hotel (now the Royal George), the Coronation Restaurant, and H.T. Midwood's Chemists.

ST PAULS CHURCH.   RAMSEY.

Prior to the consecration of St Paul's in 1832, Ballure Chapel was the only church in Ramsey, although the rapid growth in population made the provision of a larger, more conveniently sited church a matter of urgency. This photograph of St Paul's dates to about 1900, and shows the church prior to alterations and the removal of the railings, with the lamp standard and fountain complete with their surrounding steps. The inscription on the standard, erected by public subscription, commemorates 'Ramsey Incorporated 1865', the year when the local authority was inaugurated.

For many years an inshore wind coinciding with a high tide would send water pouring into Church Street, and occupants of houses and shops always had to have sandbags to hand to protect their property. This Midwood card shows a winter flood in 1920. On the left of the picture is the wall surrounding St Paul's Church, while the car is positioned opposite the entrance to St Paul's Church Hall on the right.

This photograph, taken by G. B. Cowen, shows the area to the rear of the first Catholic Church on the South Promenade, just prior to demolition. The pole on the left is at the entrance to Mona Street, with the first gateway leading to Aldritts' yard. The next gateway seaward led to the stables of coal porter Philip Crowe, and the next gate, before the building immediately behind the church, led to the scrapyard of Pat and Jane Duffy. The building by the church was a store for William Corkill, grocer and wine merchant, who had his shop in nearby Dale Street.

THE OLD BUILDINGS & OLD CATHOLIC CHURCH, RAMSEY, I.O.M.

Father Richard Barton, the parish priest, campaigned long and hard to enable the fine new Gilbert Scott designed St Maughold's to be constructed. Sadly, he died in 1908 before it could be completed. This second view shows the demolished buildings with just the gable of the old church still standing. A lot of the old stone seems to have been stacked ready for re-use.

PULLING DOWN THE OLD CATHOLIC CHURCH & BUILDINGS RAMSEY, I.O.M.

Here Archbishop Downey from Liverpool celebrates confirmation with a group of children at St Maughold's in 1929.

The Salvation Army 'barracks' stood on Church Street almost opposite the old national school and alongside L. D. Cowell's shop. Here, T.H. Midwood has photographed the local band, always an integral part of the Army.

A view of College Street, 1905, with the Independent Methodist Church on the right and Douglas Lane running off to the left. Alas, only the entrance to the street remains today, but at the time this picture was taken it led to the back of Waterloo Road with a left-hand turn at the Church Institute, continuing south to join the Old Cross; at one time Ramsey's market place. The town's grammar school, town offices and court house were all formerly sited on the street.

This view, also from 1905, shows Market Lane looking towards Church Street. The lane linked College Street with the Market Place and contained a toffee shop kept by Thomas Killip, who became parish clerk of Maughold.

This would have been a typical scene in the days when fish were loaded onto the quay for auction. Mrs Betsy Kinnin is pictured in her cap and apron on the right of the picture, a familiar figure for many years at her fish stall on the market place. John Corkish, poulterer, is the tall figure with his hands in his pockets, and William, Joe and Teddy Kinnin are also in the group at the harbour edge. The Kinnin family have been connected with fishing and the lifeboat in Ramsey for generations.

An auction takes place at the top of the Fish Steps on the quay, c1907. The fish, large cod and some skate in this photograph, would be brought up the steps two at a time and laid out in rows for inspection. At other times mackerel would be displayed for sale, often with bare patches visible on the side where the fishermen had cut off a slice for bait.

The number of schooners, smacks, ketches and small steamers visible in old photographs of Ramsey Harbour indicate an active trade. A fleet of rowing boats were always ready for hire during the holiday season and a boat also ferried passengers between the harbour piers until recent times.

Some familiar businesses can be seen on this 1930 card of the West Quay, including the Trafalgar and Stanley Hotels, Lay Brothers, and the Isle of Man Bank. The three fishing boats are typical of the period, measuring about eighteen feet long, with mast and sail but no motive power. The crew generally numbered three or four and boats normally went out in the evening to 'shoot the lines', which were left overnight, the markers often being inflated sheepskins coated with tar.

This Midwood card shows the *Manx Girl*, a half-decker well known in Ramsey early this century. She was sailed by the Corkish family for a long period and can be seen here entering the harbour by the north breakwater.

The half-decker *Caribou*, skippered by Jack Clarey, passes the swing bridge with the salt works visible in the background. Built at Peel c1910, she was converted from a yacht for fishing purposes early in the First World War. Returning to port with an overnight catch one morning, she spotted the first submarine ever seen in Ramsey Bay. During the day the *Caribou* gave free trips to sightseers, and many locals remember their first ever trip to sea as being aboard her.

Another frequent visitor to Ramsey was the S.S. *Ellan Vannin*. Originally built for the Manx fleet in 1860 as a paddle steamer with the name *Mona's Isle (II)*, she was converted into a twin screw vessel and renamed in 1883. *Ellan Vannin* regularly serviced the port of Ramsey on passage to Glasgow, Liverpool and Whitehaven, carrying cargo, passengers and the mail, and was

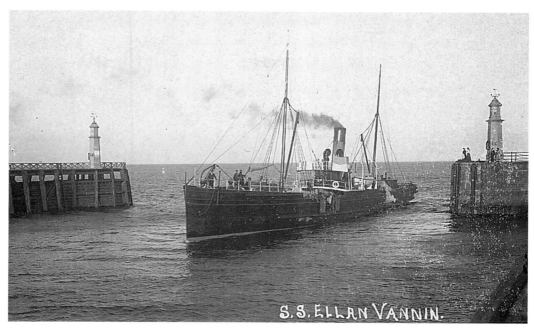

making the journey to Liverpool when she sank in the Mersey Bay with the loss of all life on 3rd December 1910. There were 21 crew and 14 passengers on board, the majority of the latter coming from Ramsey and district. A disaster fund was set up for the widows and the many orphans. The board of enquiry held after the disaster concluded that the cause was unprecedented waves of twenty-four feet, combined with the worst ever weather experienced in the Mersey Bay.

Wright of Bootle captures the holiday spirit as a bearded gentleman sporting a fine looking blazer watches the disembarking of passengers from the *Manx Fairy*. These visitors are likely to have come on a day trip from Douglas, stopping on the way at Dhoon Beach or Laxey.

The East Quay in June 1905, with a steamer unloading some farm equipment and a number of fine looking horses bound for the volunteers' camp at Milntown. Ramsey Harbour had a large export trade in farm produce at this time, and the Foxdale Mining Company imported timber and coals and shipped their ore from here. The Ramsey Quay Tramway played an important role, connecting with the steam railway. Although little used in later years, the rails were only finally lifted in the 1950s.

Another view of the volunteers' horses landing on the East Quay, this time dated 1904. The Isle of Man Steam Packet buildings can be seen in the background. They were first leased by the company in 1885, and comprised stables and warehouses as well as offices. Parts of the property were sub-let over the years, the warehouse going in 1972 when the company ceased its cargo service to Ramsey. Note the traction engine on the extreme left, a sight still to be seen on occasion in Ramsey today.

This photograph has been taken just around the corner from the previous picture and shows the warehouse buildings on the corner of the South Promenade, near the Prince of Wales Hotel. The building on the left subsequently became the Ramsey coastguard station. The year is 1920 and the cars and chauffeurs are lined up in preparation to take the royal party on their tour of the island. No chances were being taken on running short of spare tyres!

The Prince of Wales hotel, formerly the Neptune, was completely rebuilt and reopened on 16th June, 1884. Described as the prettiest on the Isle of Man, this early view shows the short-lived but very attractive glass verandah. The building, though no longer an hotel is otherwise largely unchanged, although the Neptune bar at the rear was demolished some years ago. The Albert Hotel, demolished in 1900 can be seen in the distance.

Fashions at the turn of the century left a little to be desired in their suitability for the beach. This group has been photographed by the Old Cross slipway which disappeared in the reconstruction of the South Promenade, when it was widened and renamed Queen's Promenade in 1953. Sand castles were known locally as a 'gyppys'.

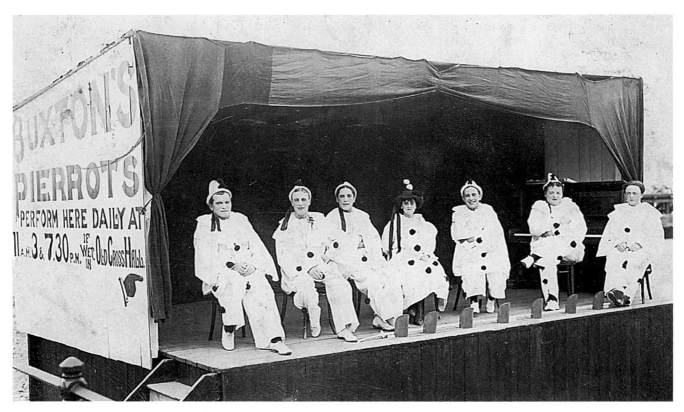

Fred Buxton was probably the greatest Manx showman, and the 'operatic pierrots' he established on Douglas Promenade in 1900 remained the most famous of the many troupes operating in the island. A Buxton's troupe was quickly established in Ramsey and they appeared three times daily on the beach by the South pier, or in the Old Cross Hall if wet. Later, the Cosy Corner became their usual location for many years.

Norman Langford was a popular comic and show manager, appearing in Ramsey over a period of many years. This 1913 card shows his entertainers, billed as the Manx Mascots after the war. Fred Buxton, who erected the Cosy Corner before the war, brought in Norman to run the concert party there, and in the twenties his entertainers appeared successfully at Ramsey's Queen's Hall for several years.

This busy scene on the South Promenade by the Imperial Hotel was sent by a holidaymaker in 1913. The American Bowling Saloon was run by the Lloyd family. Arthur Hadley's billiards saloon was also nearby, on the south side of the Cosy Corner site. Arthur was a man of many parts – photographer, town commissioner, and pioneer of the labour movement.

This fine Midwood photograph shows four Ramsey lifeboat men with a total service of over a hundred and sixty years between them. From left to right they are – Harry Sharpe, wearing the Sea Gallantry medal (in service 1888-1928, bowman 1918-28), Oscar Corlett (1875-1931, chief launcher 1901-31), Keppel Gawne (forty years as crewman), and Harry Corkish (crewman for about forty years and first coxswain 1903-25).

The crew of the *Mary Isabella II* in their heavy cork lifejackets, c1900. From 1906 lighter kapok filled jackets were introduced. The men shown include Harry Corkish (coxswain), E. Corlett, F. Corlett, Oscar Corlett, J. Crix (Bowman), J. Garret, and P. Sharpe.

The *Mary Isabella II* being launched using the haul-off warp (the rope attached to the bow of the boat). The figure in cap watching is branch secretary E.C. Kerr, who retired in 1907 after twenty-six years service. *Mary Isabella II* served from 1896-1915, taking part in forty-eight services and saving a hundred and fifty three lives.

Crowds at a lifeboat day ceremony gather to watch the launch of the boat, always the high spot of the season. This picture clearly shows T.H. Midwood's studio next to the Norbury boat house, complete with photographer and equipment on the verandah. Midwood was long associated with the lifeboat, and was chairman of the committee from 1916 until his death in 1927.

South Promenade, from T. A. Fargher's stores to Rushen House in the distance, showing the old cross slipway, with Strand Street to the rear. 'Church Parade' on a Sunday meant a particularly busy scene, with locals and visitors alike in their best clothes. Fargher's shop catered for visitors, selling beach toys and fishing tackle, and also served as the Queen's Pier Post Office for some years prior to its demolition.

A typical winter's storm scene at Ramsey in the early years of the century. The photograph was taken from the Queen's Pier, looking north along the promenade. Opening for business must have been impossible for the shops situated on the front on these occasions.

This aerial view shows much of the area lost to the South Ramsey redevelopment of the 1960s. The Old Cross slipway is on the left, with the Cosy Corner and the site of the new swimming pool on the right. Lough House on Approach Road, visible in the centre background, is the only surviving building within the area bordered by Queen's Drive to the south and Waterloo Road to the west.

As well as topographical subjects, Midwood also captured the townsfolk of Ramsey on camera. These two pictures were taken outside his photographic shop. The person on the right is Philip Corlett, Bellman from 1902 to 1927.

A group of tailors pose for the camera, probably the workers of J. Lay and Company.

A Johnson Stores' delivery boy.

Paper boys on the South Promenade.

How many men did it take to build a fine house? Here Midwood supplies the answer, but who are the men and what is the house?

Today we take bathroom scales for granted, but at one time it was possible to make a living – during the holiday season at least – by positioning a machine in a busy area such as on the promenade. This card, dated July 1911, shows John Edwin Ellison, aged twenty-three, with his magnificent new Avery weighing machine.

The Ramsey Male Choir was formed in 1917 and enjoyed early success, winning first prize at the Music Guild in April 1923. The conductress was Miss A.E. Collins and the accompanist Miss Bessie Christian. In 1931 the choir were successful both at the Guild and the Blackpool Festival, and they won more prizes in 1939, when this Midwood photograph was taken. Miss Collins, still conductress at this time, can be seen behind the teddy bear.

There have been many bands in Ramsey this century besides the official town band. The friendly societies usually supported a band and the commissioners always encouraged those that performed for visitors during the season. The Ramsey Municipal Orchestra, photographed during the thirties, were a smaller ensemble ideal for an afternoon's entertainment in the Mooragh park.

Ramsey Market Square was a focal point for all those living in the north of the island. One photographer, Wright of Bootle, visited the Ramsey area at the turn of the century and this is one of his atmospheric studies, although one wonders how much he paid those children to pose for him!

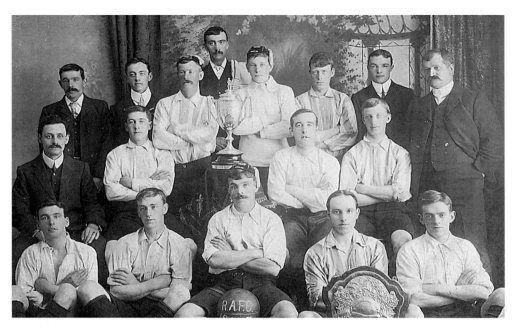

This photograph shows the triumphant 1907 Ramsey F.A. Cup winning team.
Members of the team included: L. Evans; Jas Halsall; F. Corlett; Charles Midwood;
J. Shepherd; B.W. Corkill; J. Corkish; and E. Richmond (captain). The match was
played at Peel, and Ramsey easily beat St. Mary's 6-2 with goals from Kerruish (2),
Corkill, Richmond (2) and Midwood. Local photographer Arthur Hadley can be
seen on the right of the back row.

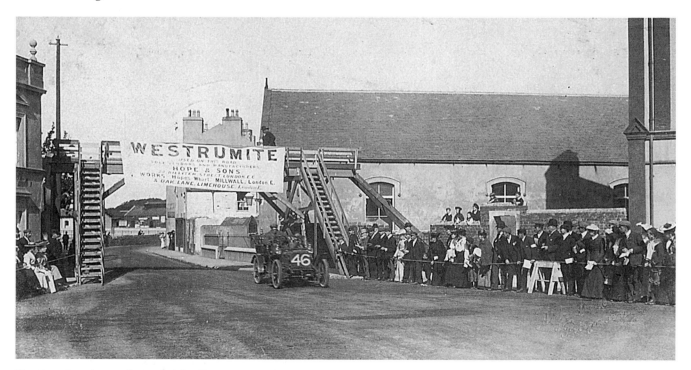

Ramsey has formed part of the Tourist Trophy course since the first race (which was for motor cars) in 1905.
Here, Charles Friswell entertains the crowds at Parliament Square in his Peugeot. He came in 13th of the 18
finishers, covering the 208 mile race (4 circuits of 52 miles around the isle) in one minute short of 8 hours. Roads
at this time were little more than dirt tracks, hence the banner advertising WESTRUMITE, one of several
substances tried at the time to eradicate the hazards of dust.

J. GUTHRIE.
WINNER — JUNIOR T.T. 1934.

The last T.T. motor car race on the island was in 1922, but motor cyclists have been competing since 1907, and, of course, continue to do so today. Here Jimmy Guthrie passes through Parliament Square on his way to victory in the 1934 T.T, the year in which he also won the senior race. He won six T.T.'s before his untimely death in 1937 in the German Grand Prix, and completed the above race at an average speed of just under 80 mph.

A. TINKLER.
AT RAMSEY HAIRPIN.

Ramsey hairpin is a part of the course that all drivers should take seriously. A. Tinkler came 3rd in 1924 in the sidecar race, but what is he doing here?

There was a children's boating pool at the Cosy Corner, and later one in Mooragh Park, although the serious model boat sailing has always taken place at Pollydooey or on Mooragh Park lake. The boat in this picture, the *St Dennis*, was winner of the League Cup in 1928-9, 1929-30 and the Challenge Cup in 1929-30. Yachts can still be seen on the lake today, but now tend to be the smaller radio-controlled type.

May Day festivities in Ramsey were held on a grand scale in the early years of the century. Here the procession is assembling at the Pavilion (Queen's Hall). The beautifully decorated carts and carriages proceeded through the town via Queen's Drive; Promenade; Old Cross; Church Street; Market Place; Parliament Street; Christian Street; Taubman Street; and Parliament Square; returning via Parliament Street; Bourne Place; Peel Street; and Waterloo Road to the ceremonies at the Pavilion. T.H. Midwood, who published this card, was chairman of the commissioners and vice-president of the May Day committee at this time (1908 -1910).

During the procession, a grand march past was held on Market Place under the supervision of the Chief Marshall, Mr E.J. Clover, who had a grocery store there. As well as the presidents and vice-presidents, a general committee of 23 gentlemen and a ladies committee, also with 23 members, were involved, with events being organised throughout the day. Several of the fancy dress groups in the pageant can be identified in this Alfred Moore postcard, including Robin Hood and his Merry Men and a charming group in Japanese costume. May Day festivities were usually held later in the month in the hope of better weather and the presence of some visitors.

Maudie, writing in July 1904 says 'This is a snap-shot of some Grammar School Sports. Dorothy, Olive and I went to see. Can you distinguish the three of us in the left hand corner?' At this time the school was held in two twenty-six roomed boarding houses on the Mooragh Promenade, prior to a move back to Waterloo Road in 1906. A field was taken at Rheast Mooar for cricket and the annual sports.

Vera Mullineux (later Mrs Vera Marsh) was crowned Ramsey's Rose Queen in July 1930. The ceremony was held at the Leighany field, and after giving a speech in Manx, Vera was crowned by Mrs Killey, the wife of the headmaster of Albert Road School. Mr Jos. Killey is the white haired man on the left of the picture, while local reporter Sydney Boulton is standing just behind the piano. On the extreme right is Miss McAdam (seen in profile), headmistress of the infant's school, accompanied by Miss Oates, who is looking towards the camera.

Celebrations for the 50th anniversary of VE Day took place in Ramsey in May 1995, but this picture shows the victory celebrations in Ramsey on 19th July 1919. School children from Andreas are prominent in this view, parading to Parliament Square with their Andreas Parochial Board School banner and Union Jacks.

The Royal Visit of July 15th 1920, with King George V and Queen Mary meeting the crowds in Parliament Square. The group of children on the right were from Andreas School and Queen Mary can be seen speaking to the teacher, Miss Graham.

Ramsey Bridge and Harbour, I. O. M.

The swing bridge over Ramsey Harbour was part of the Mooragh development project of the 1880s. Construction was much delayed, and it was only in Whit week 1892 that foot passengers were able to use it, with the official opening following on 29th June. Mr John Dougherty of College Street was appointed bridgemaster at 22/- per week and Mr Henry Kinrade of Stanley Mount, his assistant at 18/- per week. As this Hartmann card shows, in the days before heavy traffic, the bridge was a popular meeting place.

The Pool Ballroom, later the Talk of the Town, had a chequered history but was certainly a very popular venue from its opening on May 1st 1933 up to the outbreak of the war. Its cafe looked out onto a paved sun bathing terrace, with steps leading down to the pool. Cream teas were available during the day, and in the evening more substantial meals were served around the large dance floor. The resident jazz band had an excellent reputation and Mr Norman Radcliffe was the popular M.C. and dance teacher during the thirties.

One of Ramsey's best attended summer attractions for many years was the weekly swimming gala at the open air baths on the Mooragh Promenade. This included diving contests, as well as novelty events such as the greasy pole competition and picking up plates from the bottom of the bath. The baths were opened by Manx author, Hall Caine, on August 2nd 1902

Top local swimmers such as Harry Crank – shown in this Midwood photograph – David Billington and William Boulton became local celebrities and would give exhibitions of stunts part way through the programme. These included impressive sounding items such as the submarine, motionless floating, porpoise, propeller, waltz, wheel, somersaults and the shooting torpedo.

This 1906 Alfred Moore card shows the Mooragh Promenade with the last of the boarding houses still under construction. The Grand (later the Snaefell) is visible partly built in the distance. Bathing, both from machines and tents, was said to be excellent and the promenade, 90 feet wide and three quarters of a mile long, was a favourite resort for visitors. The remaining gaps on the promenade only started to be filled in the 1990s.

The Mooragh Promenade again, but this time photographed from the north end by the miniature golf links, established in 1923 by local personality Johnny Martin. The Ramsey Bay Hotel is the building with flag flying, and was particularly popular with golfers, prospering for many years under the ownership of the Misses Clarke. In its last years the building was run by the Countrywide Holiday Association and was known as Mooragh House.

During the late twenties and early thirties, Midwoods took weekly group photographs of the visitors of local boarding houses. In 1933 the Shaftesbury, on the Mooragh Promenade (proprietor Miss E. Andrew), offered 'good catering, separate tables, home comforts and bathing from the house'.

North Shore Road has long been an important thoroughfare, sometimes being called 'the gateway to the north'. From the 1850s it gave access to the shipyard and gas works, and later the salt works. The Methodist Chapel can be seen in the distance in this c1913 view, prior to being taken over as St. Olave's Mens Institute and reading room in the 1920s. North Shore Road was extended to the sea front in the 1880s to give access to the new park and promenade.

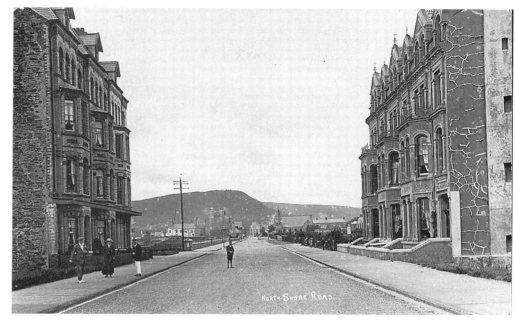

The view from the northern end of the Mooragh Park is a particularly fine one, with the 12 acre lake and winding paths decked with shrubs and flowers shown to best advantage. From 1894 the remains of the old lifeboat *The Two Sisters* could be seen on the islet in the lake, before they were eventually sold for breaking up in 1901. Early guides often commented on the lack of vegetation in the park, and it took many years for the foliage to recover from all the construction work.

The Mooragh Park bowling green has always been very popular with visitors; indeed, a green with a finer outlook would be difficult to find. The highlight of the season was always the competition for the handsome silver challenge cup presented by the Ramsey Amusements Committee. As well as the South Ramsey green by the Queen's Hall, there was also one on the South Promenade, alongside the Cosy Corner.

After the royal visit of Edward VII in 1902, much play was made of Ramsey's 'royal' status in a drive to attract visitors. The pair of swans on the Mooragh Park lake were presented by the King after his visit and they appeared on many postcards of the period. Happily, a pair of swans can still be seen in residence on the lake today.

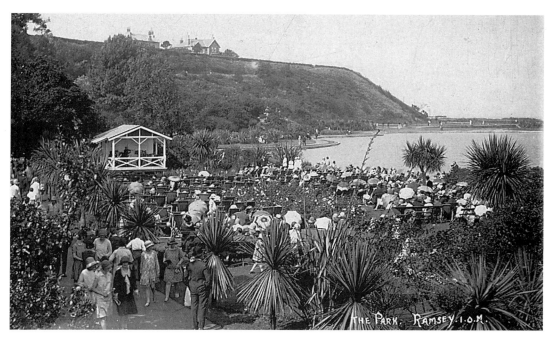

Band concerts, as now, were very popular in the park during the twenties. This view shows the famous cabbage palms to good advantage. Although they are not true palm trees and do not reach the same height that they would in their native New Zealand, the trees have nevertheless become something of a symbol for the park.

Galas and regattas were held regularly throughout the season in the Mooragh Park. A variety of boating and swimming events guaranteed a good crowd, and many people will still remember the pillow fights on a greasy pole that were a highlight of these events in more recent years.

The regatta crowd is particularly dense by the boathouse cafe, where the table containing the prizes can be seen on the left. A small charge would be made for admission to the park on such occasions, so the elevated view may not be the only reason for the number of people watching from North Shore Road!

G.B. Cowen produced this charming card of a group of well dressed girls paddling on the Mooragh. The absence of boys in the picture may suggest an outing from one of the many private schools that existed in Ramsey well into the twentieth century. Schools such as Lezayre House enjoyed success over many years, teaching primarily Ramsey girls, and it was only in 1922 that the grammar school became mixed.

Overlooking the sea at the north end of Ramsey, the Grand Island Hotel remains the largest and best known in the town. Originally the private residence of the Paton family and called Beachmount, a company was formed in October 1895 to convert the house and grounds into the first hydropathic hotel on the island. The holiday industry was developing quickly at this time and brine baths and elegant surroundings were a big attraction for the well-to-do clientele the Ramsey Hydro soon attracted. This postcard, used in 1908, shows a game of croquet in progress, a sport that has recently enjoyed a revival at the hotel.

Several businesses can be identified in this photograph of the volunteers in Parliament Street. At no. 30 John Kermode is selling Manx Ruskin Homespun from the Laxey Mills. The shop had previously been Joseph Curphey's bakery. Next door, the shoe shop is advertising Lotus Boots and Shoes, as well as 'Wood Milne Revolving Heels'. Wood Milne produced a series of postcards to give away to customers, including several Manx views.

Such a large number of cars would have been a very unusual sight in Ramsey before 1910, and they seem to have generated a considerable amount of interest. A meeting of a motor club, or a very important function at the Mitre Hotel, are the most likely explanations. The Mitre was rebuilt in 1840 and became the foremost residential hotel in the town. Wattleworth's cafe will still be fondly remembered by many.

The dedication of the Ramsey War Memorial by Bishop Denton Thompson. The Memorial, in the Court House grounds, was designed by P.M.C. Kermode in the form of a Manx cross. It was made of red Woolton sandstone and stands some twenty feet high. The front plaque on the memorial bore the inscription 'Erected in Memory of the Men of Ramsey who served in his Majesty's Forces and laid down their lives for their Country during the Great War, 1914 -1918'.

Today, Jas. Lay & Co. Ltd are one of the longest established businesses in Ramsey, working from their premises at 22 Parliament Street and formerly also at Duke Street, Douglas. At one time all garments were cut and made on the premises, and a 1909 advertisement offered gents and ladies costumes and suits made to order from 55/-. This view shows the shop windows prior to the modernisation work of the 1930s.

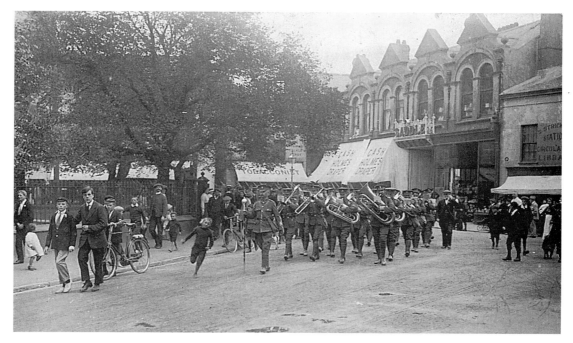

Dated 1916, this card shows a military band marching down Parliament Street and past the Saddle Buildings. Cash Holmes Draper and Strickett's Stationers and Circulating Library are visible either side of the back entrance to the Saddle Hotel. The old Saddle Inn dated back to at least 1846 and had a lane running alongside. When the present building was constructed the old right of way directly through the hotel was retained, much to the delight of generations of delivery boys.

As a political gesture, the town hall was constructed on the boundary line dividing the parishes of Maughold and Lezayre, and this picture shows the building complete with its clock, added in 1911. The building to the left of the hall, now the electricity showrooms, was still the chapel of the New Connection Methodist Church

at the time this picture was taken. The shop adjoining Parliament Square was formerly Faragher's grocers, the business being taken over in 1910 by Edward Harrison and later run by his son, Joe.

Ramsey's combined town hall and fire station were built in 1888-89 and demolished in 1972 to make way for a new building, now itself under threat. Until 1928 the Ramsey Fire Brigade operated a manual engine and hose cart, only receiving the Merryweather Hatfield engine in this picture on September 26th of that year. The engine was second hand but served the town well for ten years. Left to right can be seen Mr Edward Wilkinson (surveyor), Mr W.E. Faragher (Town Clerk), Mr J.N. Richdale, Mr J.B. Kee, Mr J.P Purcell and Mr J.J. Faragher.

This second Midwood card was also taken at the handing over ceremony. The uniformed officers in the photograph are: BACK ROW: C. Griffiths, C. Parry, C. Curphy; MIDDLE ROW: J. Gawne, W. Corlett, J. Joughin, H.I. Sayle, A Quayle, W. Christian, F. Ellison, J.R. Dugdale; FRONT ROW: J. Craine, P. Murphy, J. Cottier, John Smith (chief officer) and J.W. Sayle. Robert Cain was appointed driver of the new motor engine, the first on the Island.

The parish church of Lezayre, consecrated in 1835, was designed by John Welch, the famous architect of the Tower of Refuge, King William's College, and the Smelt Memorial in Castletown. The view from the main road has changed little over the years, although the presence of the War Memorial places this Midwood card in the inter-war period.

Here, T.H. Midwood gives some idea of the sheer size of the Milntown volunteers camps with their tents stretching into the distance on both sides of Lezayre Road. Camps were usually held in May or late June and could last several weeks. The arrival of the volunteers meant good business for the railway and a temporary Milntown Camp Station was erected from 1908, served by extra, late trains.

Sunday service at the camp, here attended by the officers and their ladies. As can be seen from the finery of the ladies clothing, they enjoyed rather better conditions than their men. Note the pulpit made from drums! In the 1920s, Field-Marshal Montgomery, then a young officer in camp with the Territorials in fields along the Bride Road, patronised the Ramsey Hydro.

The volunteers in 1905, marching along Lezayre Road near to Milntown with the camp visible on both sides of the road. Milntown was the seat of the Christians, most famous of all the Manx families. William Christian (Iliam Dhone) and Fletcher Christian (of Mutiny on the *Bounty* fame) have been the best known members.

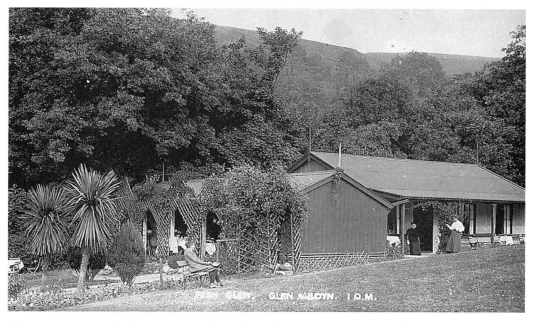

The tea rooms and pleasure grounds at Fern Glen in the upper reaches of Glen Auldyn were run by James Lindsay and for 1/- each way (later reduced to 6d) a regular bus service ran from Ramsey's market square. A steep zig-zagging path ascended into the heart of the glen where a lovely little waterfall that rejoiced in the name of Niagara could be seen.

Glen Auldyn has experienced flooding in recent years, but the worst incidence on record occurred on the night of September 18th, 1930. The downpour began at midnight and nearly four and a half inches of rain fell in a few hours. All the streams rising in the neighbourhood of Snaefell became raging torrents and areas of flat land were transformed into huge lakes. Enormous trees were carried down the glen and some became wedged under the railway bridge at Milntown, moving it some inches and preventing trains running into Ramsey for several days.

All the foot-bridges in Glen Auldyn were swept away during the floods, as was the stone bridge at the junction of the two streams. The roadways in the upper glen and at Milntown were carried away completely, the post office in the glen was mired in a sea of mud with rabbit hutches floating around the garden, and the story is often told of how a large wooden gate from a house at the top of the glen was found at Port Mooar in Maughold. Sulby and Laxey were also very badly hit by flooding on this occasion.

In the days before newspapers regularly carried photographs, postcards featuring local events such as floods, accidents or shipwrecks were very popular. These cards would be printed in very small numbers, often being rushed out on the same day as the incident depicted. The vehicle in difficulties here looks rather like the original Fern Glen bus, but the authors would be pleased to hear of any details of the incident.

Ramsey Golf Club was formed in September 1891, and as the Town Guide claimed for many years, had the honour of introducing golf to the Isle of Man. The original course was laid out by the veteran Tom Morris and soon proved so popular that an extension was essential. The services of John Morris of Hoylake were secured and the full eighteen hole course was opened by the Lieutenant Governor, Lord Raglan, in 1907.

The extension made the links more central to the town, with the creation of an entrance to the new club house on Brookfield Road. Originally of a rather easy playing nature, the course was re-modelled during the winter of 1929-30 by the world famous golfer, James Braid. The first hole, shown here prior to this, was a dog-leg of 533 yards with a burn running almost the full length of the fairway on the right hand side, and the green on the other side of the burn.

Boating on the Sulby River was a very popular pastime with visitors earlier in the century, as this view taken at the White Bridge shows. Local children would wait to pull the visitors' row boats over the rapids – a well-paid service, while a Mr Rae had a refreshment stand on the riverside from which he invited passing boats to pull in and enjoy a lemonade or ginger beer. Today, the rowing boats have disappeared but the area is still popular, and in 1995 a new nature trail was opened at nearby Poylldooey.

Albion Terrace on Lezayre Road has a particularly fine facade and has recently been nominated to be listed for its architectural merit. Built in 1847 by the Reverend John Buck, the houses were advertised for sale the following year by William Clucas, a local surgeon. The terrace appears at its best in this T.H. Midwood view from the 1920s.

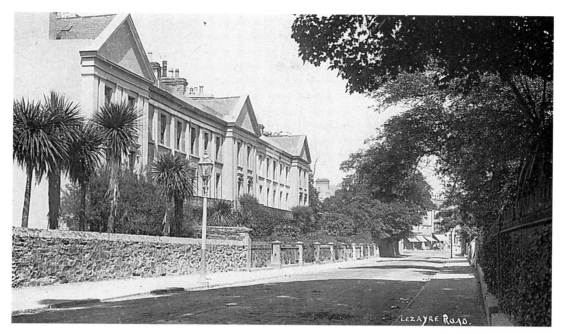

Chrystal Brothers Auctioneers are the oldest business in Ramsey remaining in the hands of the same family. In the 1880s Chrystal Brothers were, among other things, mineral water manufacturers in Bowring Road, premises which have been used as the Ramsey Mart for many years. On mart days people would come in from the country by horse-drawn cart, bicycle or train. Horses could be left at stables such as Livesey's in Water Street, and shops would stay open until late – even midnight in the case of Callow's grocers in Church Street.

The railway station at Ramsey was built in 1878 on land adjacent to the Sulby River, partly on a former timber yard. The building was quite a large affair, designed to include the head offices of the Manx Northern Railway, and like all the other buildings at the Ramsey terminus it was constructed by local builders, Boyde Brothers. Its position on the edge of town always tended to give it a deserted appearance, especially in later years when few trains ran on the Ramsey line.

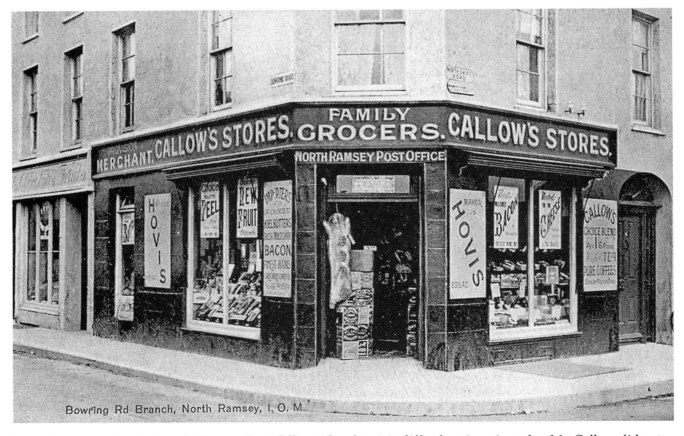

There is no one about at North Ramsey Post Office either, but it is difficult to imagine what Mr. Callow did not sell, and the shop promises not to be deserted for long!

The Riverside Estate, originally known as Port Natal, is situated just up river from the Bowring Road stone bridge. It was developed on meadowland in the late 1850s by Daniel Callow, a Ramsey mason and builder, and extended as far as the Bridge Inn, which he built for his daughter, Mrs Eleanor Christian.

Completed in 1862, St Olave's Church was consecrated on 20th April 1881 and dedicated to St Olaf, Patron Saint of Norway. It is built in the Early English Decorated style, using local stone incorporating red Whitehaven sandstone. This photograph shows the church with the original stone cross on the west gable and iron spire on the belfry tower – both replaced over the years due to storm damage. Many of the elm trees have been removed over the years, as their proximity to the building threatened structural damage.

The opening of the Ramsey Cottage Hospital on 23rd July 1907 met a real need for a hospital in this area. Originally having ten beds, it was built and run on voluntary donations, including those from the Henry Bloom Noble Trust.

The Ramsey Children's Home and Orphanage was established at Ballacloan, alongside North Shore Road, on September 1st 1880, and owed its origins to the nearby Suzannah Gibson Refuge for Destitute Children. Twenty-nine children were originally accommodated, although in 1917 the Dalmeny Hydro was bought to take the girls, leaving thirty-five boys at Ballacloan.

This 1913 postcard of Windsor Mount was sent by a holiday-maker staying at Mrs Griffith's Park Crest (marked by a cross). The National Children's Home is on the left. Originally built as a house for the Gibson family, the shipyard owners, it was still 'mixed' at this time, becoming the boys' home shortly afterwards, and remaining so until 1956. Ramsey Football Club bought the property in 1958

and used the house as changing rooms and committee accommodation until their stadium was extended in the 1980s. Ballacloan has now been converted into flats.

Windsor Road presents a charming picture in this 1913 view. The terrace above the road, Victoria Place, was built in the 1830s although the opposite side was not developed until the 1860s, when new houses were individually built in a variety of styles according to James Corlett's plans. The Coronation Tennis Courts, a favourite meeting place for the well-to-do in the inter-war years, were to be found at the Bowring Road end of Windsor Road.

The Manx Electric Railway Station was built on the site of Elm Villa, the model for Pete Quilliam's Ramsey house in Hall Caine's *The Manxman*. In this 1905 view the station looks very attractive, with its charming gardens and kiosks. The Station Bar was situated in the Palace until it was rebuilt and renamed the Plaza in 1935.

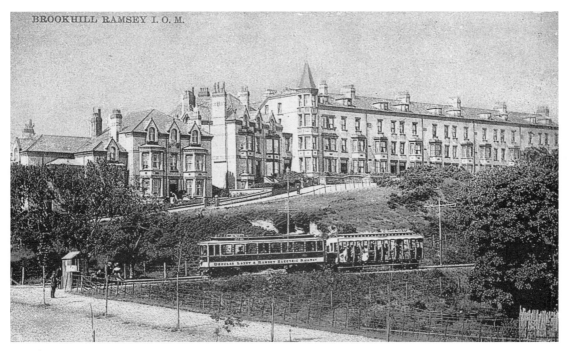

Baur's published this card of Brookhill in 1905. It shows the M.E.R. halt there, soon after the line through to the Ramsey terminus was opened in 1899. The closed car bears the new 'Douglas, Laxey and Ramsey Electric Railway' livery. Coal destined for Ballaglass Power Station was loaded at Queen's Drive using a portable ramp. Queen's Drive continued past the pavilion to the junction of the Crescent Road, although prior to 1913 there was no Leaney Road to link it up with May Hill.

The newly refurbished Plaza Cinema, 1936. Manx Picturedromes opened the Palace as a cinema as early as 1912, but it enjoyed little success until it reopened under new management on 26th July, 1920. The programme on that night included 'The Pawnshop' starring Charlie Chaplin, along with items from the Ramsey Male Choir and Norman Longford's pierrots. The former Dumbell's Bank, in the days after the removal of its tower, is on the right.

The Britannia Hotel was formerly called the Waterloo. Originally constructed in 1847 as a private house with stables at the back, it was converted into a hotel in 1909 by one John Nelson. He was a total abstainer, although his son, Bob, was licensee of the Trafalgar Hotel for many years.

The Wesleyan Methodist Chapel on Waterloo Road was constructed in 1845, and the first services held on July 5th, 1846. This G.B. Cowen card dates from c1912, soon after the interior had been re-seated and the vestibule and new windows added. Posters were often to be seen pasted on the wall advertising forthcoming events. The presence of the tree right in the middle of Parsonage Road is a charming reminder of the lack of motor traffic at this time!

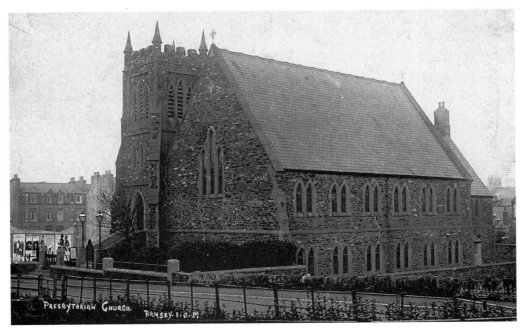

The Presbyterian Church in Ramsey has always been known as the 'Scotch Kirk'. Originally, Scots in the area held meetings in a barn on the swimming pool site, before moving to the building in Albert Street that later became Quayle's Hall in 1834. The new church in Waterloo Road was opened in 1885, and cost in the region of £2,300. As part of the fund-raising effort, Joe Mylchreest, the 'Diamond King', chaired a concert and donated £25.

The Albion Hotel closed down in the 1930s and was taken over by the Friendship Holiday Association, who used it, along with the nearby Queen's Hall as a recreational centre. Now known as Ascog Hall, the building was used to billet soldiers guarding the Mooragh Internment Camp during the war. The entrance into the main bar of the Albion is visible on this card, and there were also side doors on Stanley Mount East and Stanley Mount West.

Ballure Road was built in 1764, and prior to this the only public right of way was along the broughs, turning inland by the present day Beach Hotel car park. The majority of the houses on the road took guests when this photograph was taken in 1907, and names such as Marlborough House, Woodville, and of course Mona Ville (later the Beach) were familiar to generations of holidaymakers.

The Queen's Hotel had a long history in Ramsey's tourist industry, having been built in 1886 to coincide with the opening of the Queen's Pier. It was constructed by local builders Callows, on a sandy site known as Starkey's Cronk. The owner of the Queen's was Mr John Kneale, and ownership remained in his family until 1968. While Mr Kneale was in Africa the hotel was let to a Mrs Wild for some years up to 1913, the period of this Midwood photograph. The Queen's burnt down in April 1983.

The oldest building in Ramsey, Ballure Chapel, stands on the site of an ancient Keeill. It has fallen into ruin on several occasions, and was restored most recently in 1851. On the west side of the Chapel, in the rather neglected churchyard, the graves of Martha and Elizabeth Fricker, sisters of the wives of the poets Southey,

Coleridge and Lovel, can still be seen. This card, used in 1907, dates from before Canon Harrison purchased and planted the field in front of the chapel to improve its appearance. Formerly, a stream ran by the chapel, and the lower portion of Queen's Drive on the way to Ballure was known as 'The Bog'.

For many years, bathing north of the Ballure stream was segregated into three areas set aside for ladies, gentlemen, and – in between – an area for ladies intending to bathe with gentlemen! All bathers were required to wear the regulation combination costume covering the body from shoulder to the knee. Bathing machines, with horse in attendance, were a feature of Ballure Beach up to 1914.

Gathering seaweed on Ballure Beach. As early as 1812, Thomas Quayle commented on the use of seaweed to improve the land for the production of spring corn, and until comparatively recent times, where farms were situated adjacent to the shore, the practice continued. Indeed, it was once common to see cows grazing on the beach in parts of the Island – doubtless with some effect on the taste of the milk!

The view from below Albert Tower before 1910 indicates the extent of the growth of Ramsey over the last ninety years. There is only one building on Beaumont Road, and Eskdale stands alone on the upper part of Queen's Drive. The row of lock-up shops built by the sea end of Queen's Drive can be seen, and on the right hand edge of the photograph, the tennis courts next to the Queen's Hall.

An electric car, with trailer and parcels van, crosses Ballure Bridge on its way to Douglas, c1930. The gardens above Ballure Glen have yet to be developed but Ballure Cottage can just be seen among the trees on the left. This cottage was formerly the seat of the Christians of Ballure and the fuchsia tree in the garden was thought to be the biggest in the world at this time.

Ballure Bridge was built at a cost of £35 in 1787 in response to pleas by local residents worried by the dangers of crossing the ford at this spot – something that would have been necessary to attend church, for example. A temporary tramway terminus was established here in July 1898, while a second bridge was constructed over

the glen parallel with the road bridge. Snow scenes of Ramsey are rarely seen on postcards, although the use of such cards at Christmas was quite widespread.

In the days before the construction of Ballure Bridge, travellers were forced to climb the hills to cross the river at a safer point. The 'old Douglas Road' did not follow the current route but went by a path higher up the glen, on the right hand side, crossing the stream and continuing to the Hibernia. The lower road up Ballure glen was constructed with the development of the reservoirs in the 1860s.

The people of Ramsey had to get their water from wells or streams until a water act in 1859 led to the formation of a water company. Provision was still on a limited scale until 1885, when a large new reservoir was opened in Ballure Glen. Although no longer in use and overgrown, the reservoir shown in this 1930s Midwood view can still be seen today.

'Old Pete' was undoubtedly the most famous of Ramsey characters, achieving a degree of national fame in the years after Hall Caine's *The Manxman* appeared in 1894. Pete was really John Kennish (known also as Jackie Hoodin or Jackie Ballure), and inadvertently became famous after G.B. Cowen took a photograph of his quaint cottage to illustrate an American edition of the book. To obtain better light for the photograph it is said that Cowen had a hole knocked in the cottage wall! Jackie was a great character, with a self-taught encyclopaedic knowledge of many subjects, and his cottage soon became a stopping place for all the local visitors and carriage parties.

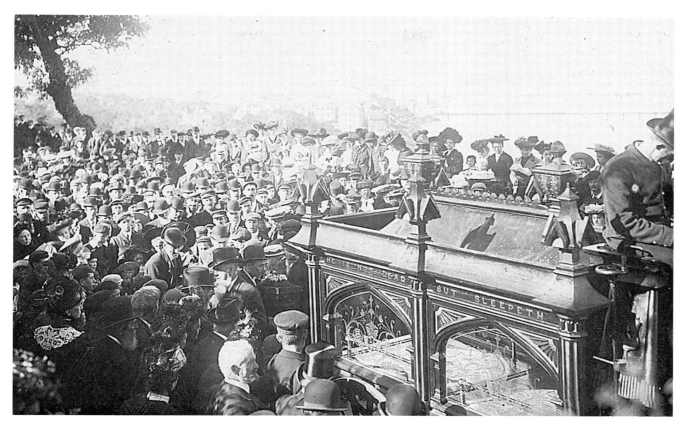

Lame from early boyhood, Jackie nevertheless became a gardener by trade, and later took to carpentry, making spinning wheels and knick-knacks to sell to visitors. He died on September 20th 1906, having been ill with diabetes, and his funeral was one of the best attended in the history of the town. This Midwood view, taken outside his single room cottage (which stood near the water trough on the right hand side going up the hill from Ballure Bridge), gives some idea of the high esteem in which he was held. Postcards of 'Pete' and his cottage continued to be produced for many years after his death.

When this postcard was sent in May 1904 the road around the hairpin bend was still referred to as the 'new road from Ramsey'. The writer of this card says 'This is one of the corners that the racing cars have to go round'. The first Gordon Bennett trials, to choose three British representatives for the International Gordon Bennett Cup, took place on May 14th, attracting an entry of eleven cars. At this time there were reckoned to be only two cars on the whole Island!

ALBERT TOWER.   RAMSE

Albert Tower was erected by public subscription to commemorate the royal visit of 1847 by Queen Victoria and Prince Albert. The tower, 45 feet high and constructed of blue mountain slate laced with South Barrule granite, marks the spot where Prince Albert stood to admire the view of the town. It is many years since visitors were able to climb it or buy refreshments there, but the tower remains a local landmark and very much a symbol of Ramsey.

Elfin Glen is a charming little gorge to the west of Albert Tower. The entrance is by the Hairpin Bend, with the path leading up to the Mountain Road slightly above the tower. Originally known as Ballacowle Glen, the area was given its English name in the nineteenth century as a ploy to attract holiday-makers, so important to the economy of the town.

ELFIN GLEN.

The scenery on the Mountain Road above Albert Tower remains as unspoilt today as it is on this 1933 Valentine's card. The road surface however, has certainly improved. For many years after the T.T. races moved to the mountain circuit, the 'road' was mostly only rutted farm tracks, with obstacles such as gates and wandering farm animals to be negotiated. It was only in the 1920s that conditions started to improve, and the roads were only finally closed for practices in 1928.

This view of Port Lewaigue dates from 1911 and shows a short section of the promenade that was intended to stretch all the way to Ramsey. The remains of a breakwater, built of large stones with posts sticking out, on which mooring ropes for boats could be tied, can also be seen. The breakwater was built to give shelter to sailing boats bringing limestone from Castletown to the many small lime kilns in the parish.

Port-e-Vullen lies just to the south of Port Lewaigue, separated by the headland of Gob ny Rona. The Port-e-Vullen Residential Hotel and others such as Min-e-Don made this a popular area with holiday makers seeking a quiet retreat. Before the First World War there was a tea-room with rowing boats for hire, run under the management of the Richardson family.

Port-e-Vullen was formerly called Port-e-Myllin or 'Port of the Mill', and at the turn of the century the remains of the old mill wheel could still be seen below the small waterfall by the shore. A considerable amount of building took place around the turn of the century, when the Lewaigue Estates Company planned to develop the whole headland into a building estate with hydro and bathing pool. However, the company ran into financial difficulties in 1906, and the plans were shelved.

Sir Thomas Henry Hall Caine (1853-1931) was undoubtedly
the most successful author (in terms of books published and
fees received) to have lived on the Isle of Man.

Born in Runcorn, Cheshire, of a Manx father and
Cumbrian mother, he had a long association with the island
and lived there for the last forty years of his life. At seventeen
he came over to run the school at Maughold Head, which he
did for a year before returning to Liverpool, where he began
his literary career. It was the publication in 1887 of his third
novel, *The Deemster*, that established his reputation as a
novelist, and in particular as a Manx novelist. From then on
his titles sold in their millions, and by the turn of the century
he had taken up residence on the Island at Greeba Castle,
where he lived, between long absences, until his death in 1931.

There was always a love-hate relationship between Hall
Caine and the people of the Isle of Man. Islanders resented the
way that they were portrayed in the Manx novels, and were
offended by the coarse plots that Caine created. However, the
fame of the novels came to be appreciated as an invaluable aid
to the Manx tourist industry which was blossoming during
this period.

Hall Caine was a member of the House of Keys of
Ramsey from 1901 until 1908, and was elected on a most
radical programme, under which he presented himself as a
'man of the people'. However, for reasons of health, he was
abroad for most of this period and rarely attended sessions of
parliament.

Despite his poor health and political commitments, Caine
continued to write copiously until his death, and although almost totally forgotten now he was considered to be
one of the most important novelists of his age. His acute business sense and egotistic obsession with publicity
placed him constantly in the public eye, and his career made him a very wealthy man.

With typical vanity, Hall Caine demanded that he be buried at the top of Maughold Head, together with a
suitably large monument that could be seen for miles around on both land and sea, and with this in mind he
bought a plot of land for the purpose. However, two weeks before his death he attempted to visit his proposed

resting place,
but the journey
was beyond
him. Deciding
that if he
couldn't get to
his own burial
site, neither
would the
thousands of
visitors he
anticipated, he
thus settled for
a more modest
burial plot and
monument in
the consecrated
ground of
Maughold
churchyard.

This fine early Midwood photograph shows Maughold church prior to 1854, with the Roolwer Cross in the middle of the village green. In that year the famous local antiquary, P.M.C. Kermode, had it moved inside the churchyard for safety. The 14th century parish cross, visible by the church entrance, had to wait until 1937 to be moved away from the dangers of motor traffic. The thatched cottage on the left still survives, but the one on the right was soon to be replaced by a sturdily built house. Note the traces of snow in the photograph.

The view from the road to Maughold lighthouse, looking across to North Barrule, is claimed by many to be the finest on the island. It also reveals the full extent of Maughold churchyard, which is the largest on the Island. It was once fortified, and contains the ruins of three early keeills, with the site of a fourth also recorded. The cross-house, to the right of the main entrance, contains the largest collection of Celtic and Norse crosses on the island.

Maughold Lighthouse was only opened on 15th April 1914, following a long campaign for its construction. Before this, this dangerous stretch of coast was protected by the Bahama Bank Lightship. The road to the lighthouse did not exist at the time the lighthouse became operational, and was constructed with some difficulty afterwards, starting from between the church gate and the parish cross. The lighthouse looks newly constructed in this view and the men on the top may well have been performing some sort of 'topping-out' ceremony. Recently, the light has been made fully automatic.

Although Port Mooar has a fine large harbour, it has only been used by local fishermen and farmers since the importing of lime stopped in the 18th century. In this 1905 picture Port Mooar Cottage can still be seen on the beach in a good state of repair. The cottage was the home of Jackie Kermode, famous for his rendering of the Dirk Dance of the Kings of Mann.

By the thirties, Port Mooar reached the height of its popularity as a short excursion from Ramsey, accessible to a new generation of car owners. A wooden building on the beach was opened as a cafe by George Logan, an enterprising personality who at one time lived in a caravan by the Hairpin Corner. The cafe was destroyed by fire during the fifties, and the site now forms part of the garden of what is still the only house on the beach today.

Ballajora has changed little in the ninety years since this picture was taken. Here the Manx Electric Railway halt is to the right, and the top of the mail box (emptied by the M.E.R. until the 1970s) can just be seen. The most notable omission, looking past Port Mooar into the distance, is the absence of Maughold lighthouse, not built until 1914.

Ballaglass Glen is less spectacular than the Dhoon, but is the more charming of the two. The Ballaglass Falls do not descend from any great height, but form a series of cascades making their way through gaps in the rocks. Still to be seen are the remains of a flax mill, and the stone buildings of a lead mine operated by the Great Mona Mining Company from 1854-1867.

Cornaa beach is about two miles away from Ballaglass Glen – despite the caption on this Midwood card! Port Cornaa has a steepish shingle beach and was famous as the point where the telegraph cable to England entered the sea. It was also one of the inlets used for the off-loading of limestone in the nineteenth century and the ruins of a proposed Bellite (explosive) factory can be seen nearby.

The road leading down from Cornaa tram station forms a delightful rural scene in this picture by Taggart of Douglas. Cornaa Mill was positioned lower down the road on a site well served by paths and roads from all over the parish. The mill was run by the Gelling family from 1841 (or earlier), up until its closure in 1951. At the time, the old Manx hand-loom could still be seen in use in a cottage nearby.

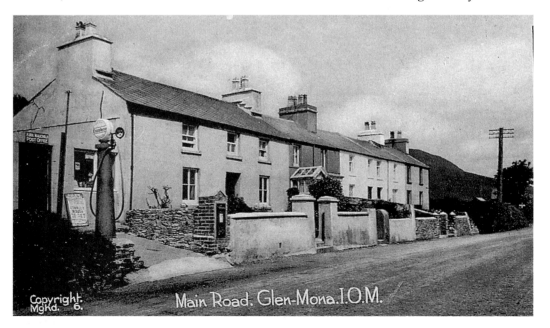

Kirk Maughold Post Office was originally housed in Hillside Cottage, Corony Hill. Members of the Corkill family were postmasters for many years, and part of the stone post box still stands in the garden there. This 1930s view shows the post office at its present site by the Glen Mona Hotel. It was kept by a Mrs Shimmin at the time. Note the wonderful Essolene petrol pump.

The Dhoon Glen Hotel was very popular with visitors arriving on the Manx Electric Railway, and also with travellers and locals on the main Ramsey to Laxey Road. On Sunday, local licensing laws decreed that only those travelling more than three miles were entitled to a drink, and as it was the nearest hotel to Ramsey, crowds would queue up for opening time! A mysterious fire on 3rd April 1932 completely destroyed the building.

The Dhoon Glen is the most spectacular on the island, although it is visited relatively little today, compared to its heyday before the First World War. This Midwood card shows the principal waterfall, which makes two leaps totalling nearly 160 feet – a magnificent sight after heavy rainfall. In its early days as a tourist attraction there was a cafe on the beach, and the pleasure steamer *Manx Fairy* would call with trippers.

In 600 years Bishopscourt has developed from a fortified peel tower to a pleasant country house. It is most famous as the residence of the Bishop of Sodor and Mann, having been restored by Bishop Wilson after he found the house in ruins on his arrival in 1698. A surprising number of postcards of Bishopscourt are signed by the Bishop – they were presumably a useful fund raiser.

Taken in July 1920, this Midwood photograph shows King George V and Queen Mary accompanied by Princess Mary at Bishopscourt. The bishop, Denton Thompson, can be seen fifth from the left, with Mr Bertram Sargeaunt, government secretary (who lived to the age of 101) on his left, and Canon C.A. Cannon, at that time Principal of the Bishop Wilson College to the left of him.

The little shop in Ballaugh, run by the Teare family, had a reputation for providing any item one could think of. Wallpaper, shoes, and dress material were all stocked, as well as the more obvious items. This was vital , as a trip into Ramsey or Peel would be a rare event indeed, perhaps undertaken only two or three times a year.

Ballaugh village before 1910 presents a very tranquil scene, with local children posing in the road for the photographer. Although not as old as some, the village is particularly pleasant, centred around a crossroads where the road from Old Ballaugh crosses the main road before passing up Ballaugh Glen. Not long before this photograph was taken, the village could boast of a hat factory and a brewery.

This picture has been taken from the same point as the last, but looking up the side road towards the Methodist Church. The church has recently celebrated its 125th anniversary but faces an uncertain future due to dwindling congregations.

Alfred Moore produced this card of the Albert Hotel in Ballaugh in 1905. The licensee, William Teare, is almost certainly the gentleman to be seen with arms folded at the door of the Inn. The shop featured in the previous two pictures can be seen in the distance, just before the crossroads and Ballaugh Bridge.

At one time each parish would have had several blacksmiths, their skills often being passed down through generations of the same family. Their work was essential to the farmer, not just in shoeing horses, but also for the repair and manufacture of farm equipment. The smithy in the photograph is a typically low structure with a slate roof and very small windows.

A cart and driver pose for G.B. Cowen in Ballaugh, c1900. The style of house shown is typical of Manx country homes of the period, which were constructed from stone, and roofed with slate rather than thatch.

The earliest (known) reference to St. Mary's de Ballaugh occurs in a papal bull of 1231, although no account can be found of the construction of this building. When a new parish church was built on a different site in 1832, the 'old' building, pictured here, fell into decay, but was rescued by Rector Rev. T. Howard who took down the chancel and had it re-roofed in 1849. The famous leaning pillars date from the 18th century and tradition has it that when they meet the end of the world has come!

Ballaugh station was the principal stop between Kirk Michael and Ramsey and had a crossing loop, as well as a cattle platform and siding with goods shed. The station building, on the left in this picture, is typical of those built by the Manx Northern Railway. Engines were sometimes exchanged between trains here, but all was quiet when this Tucks view was taken in the thirties.

Sulby Glen Hotel is the most central point for visitors to this area, and has long been an ideal stopping-off point for traffic travelling on the long route to Ramsey. It stands midway between Sulby Bridge and Gob-e-Volleh Crags, on the main road opposite to Sulby Glen, with the station located just behind it.

The bowling green shown on this 1906 postcard was behind the Sulby Glen Hotel. At the time, the well-known sporting personality Walker Anderson kept the hotel, and he introduced the green.

Valentine's published this view of Station Road, Sulby, in 1914. It shows the level crossing on the road to Jurby. Sulby Glen Station was more convenient for the village than Sulby Bridge Station, located three quarters of a mile further east, and became much busier than had been anticipated. As a result, it was rebuilt in 1910, and is in a style quite different to other stations on the line. The platform, with the awning that formed part of the frontage of the building, is just visible on the right.

A colourfully decorated cart leads a procession of Sulby school children during events held to mark the 100th anniversary of Sulby Sunday School. This G.B. Cowen postcard was sent in May 1908.

The car in this photograph would have been one of very few on the Island in 1905, and parked outside the Sulby Post and Telegraph Office it has drawn several admiring onlookers. Likely to have belonged to the photographer, the vehicle would not only have provided a convenient means of transporting equipment around, but would also guarantee a point of interest and degree of animation in his photographs.

Participants and onlookers gather on the main road in the centre of Sulby village during the local carnival, photographed by T.H. Midwood, c1905. As with many of the close-knit communities on the island, the carnival was a high point of the year.

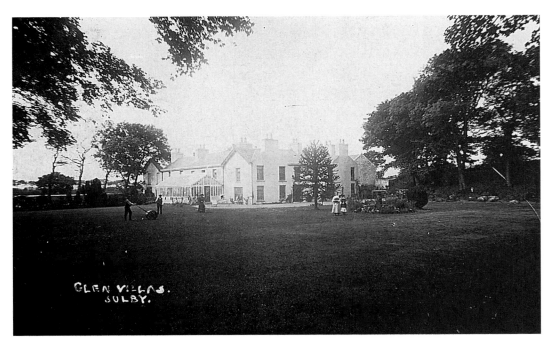

Glen Villas, Sulby, often feature on old photographs showing local events such as garden parties and fetes. At one time there was a brewery at Glen Villas, and the sediment left from beer production was allowed to run into an adjoining field called the Deigin. Environmental pollution in the countryside is not a recent problem!

Thatched cottages had become something of a curiosity by the turn of the century, and photographers made a point of using them for their pictures. At the time, the old hamlet of Sulby still contained several particularly impressive thatched buildings, and Wright and Co. of Bootle have caught the mood in this fine photograph. Note the projecting stones, which were built into the walls of the house for securing the 'suggane' (twisted straw rope) which tied down the thatch.

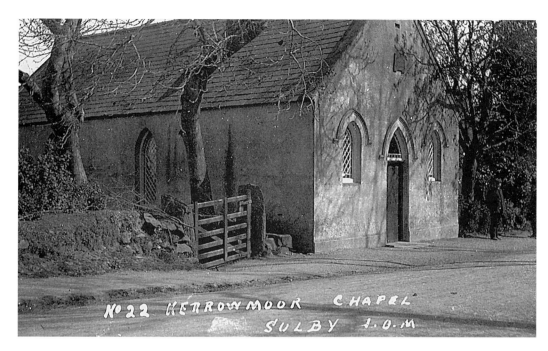

The Primitive Methodist Chapel at Kerrowmoar, Sulby, was erected in 1825, only two years after the arrival of the movement on the island. It cost £151 and seated 155 people. Travelling preachers of the time ran a programme that started at Kirk Michael on Monday, then toured Orrisdale, Ballaugh and Kerrowmoar through the week, and finished in Ramsey with a class on Friday evening.

With walls up to four feet thick, thatched cottages were warm in the winter and cool in the summer. The standard layout for these dwellings comprised a kitchen which was open up to the roof and a parlour, with a cockloft above, often used for sleeping accommodation. The thatched cottages by the banks of the river in Sulby were occupied by the well known characters Jim the Bellman, and Billie Paaie and his twelve cats.

The Sulby Claddagh is an ideal place to sit and watch the world go by. Famous as the scene of Sulby Fair, it was a delightful wilderness of gorse in the early summer. The Claddagh bridge is in the background, and to the left Cronk Sumark (Primrose Hill), an isolated grassy hill with a prehistoric earth fort situated near the summit.

The present church at Jurby was built in 1829, using material from the adjacent old building. Despite having received a lot of criticism over the years for its architectural failings, it serves as a landmark visible for many miles around, standing as it does on an elevated tract of land near the sea. It has a very attractive interior, and contains some fine Scandinavian crosses.

Although the Gothic style makes it seem older, Ballamoor Castle was only built in 1905. Standing on the site of a smaller historic house, which belonged to a branch of the Christian family, the castle was once owned by the eccentric Dr. Cannon. He was unjustly thought to be a spy, and forced to sell the house in 1939 due to its proximity to the Jurby RAF Station. Ballamoar is famous for its magnificent grounds and gardens, which cover nearly fifty acres.

St. Jude's Chapel appears thick with ivy in this early twentieth century photograph. The chapel is close to Ballachurry and was built in 1839 by public subscription. On the left of the picture is the school building, which was erected in 1854 and only closed in the 1970s. At the time this picture was taken, Miss A.I. Dodd was in charge of the school.

Andreas Post Office has moved more than once since 1863, when it was to be found 'at Frederick Radcliff's.' This photograph shows the post office in the 1920s, when it was run by the Kneale family. The postman was Jim Clegg, who took over from John Shimmin in 1902 and was paid 19/- a week. The job was very strenuous, and post had to be carried for the three auxiliaries who distributed letters in the Regaby, Smeale and St. Jude's areas.

Hall Caine Aerodrome was only in service for scheduled flights from 1935 until 1937, and fell into decline soon afterwards. Established by Ralph and Derwent Hall Caine in memory of their father, it was situated at Close Lake on the Jurby road. For 25/- one could fly to Blackpool in a 28 seater, the trip taking 45 minutes.

The much loved Archdeacon John Kewley, Rector of Andreas from 1912 to 1939, at the Andreas Root Show. This event was the oldest produce show on the island, and dated back to 1895 when Archdeacon Gill was rector. The show was first held in the coach house at the rectory, and Archdeacon Kewley was president of the committee for many years.

Many thousands of holiday makers have explored the Isle of Man on foot or bicycle, staying at its various youth hostels. Andreas Rectory (above), was once a hostel, and there were other branches at Union Mills and Colby. By the 1970s hostels were to be found at Laxey, Ramsey and Port Erin, but one by one they closed, the last to go being Axnfel at Laxey.

The present Andreas School was opened in 1903 when its headmaster was the Manx scholar Mr W. Radcliffe. This picture shows the school in 1922 when Wilfred E. Kelly was head teacher. Mr Kelly and his staff can be seen in the school grounds. The two teachers at this time were Miss M. Graham and Miss Flo Sayle.

Some of the older pupils at Andreas School, with headmaster Kelly seated on the right, photographed in 1922. Mr Kelly had previously been at Bride School and left Andreas for Rushen School in 1927.

Today, Kirk Andreas Church looks rather out of proportion, as the top half of its tower was demolished during the war by the Air Ministry in order to improve safety at the nearby airfield. St Andrew's was originally built in 1802 with a small bell turret. The bell tower, 120 feet high, was added separately in 1869, and linked to the main building by an arch. Stone for the building work had to be carried from Sulby Glen, the nearest quarry to Andreas.

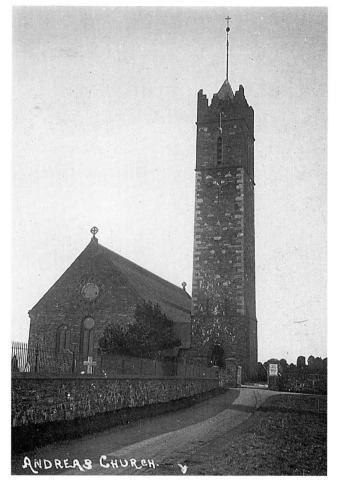

The unveiling of the Andreas War Memorial in 1922. At the time, coal boring was still taking place in the area, and a man named Kendal who worked in the mining industry designed the memorial.

Andreas choir proudly display their first prize trophy from the 1922 Music Guild. The Guild was a focus for national pride and the annual festival, held in the Palace Ballroom, Douglas, was a highlight of the island's cultural calendar.

Horticulture would have played an important part in the curriculum of a country school before the Second World War, and this photograph shows the Bride School vegetable garden, with headmaster Mr. W.E. Kelly standing in the centre and the boys working on their plots around him. The garden is now the site of the village playing fields.

Bride's new church, dedicated to St. Bridget, was consecrated in 1876 and along with its surroundings has always formed a focus for life in the parish. Palm Cottage, on the right of the picture, and the village green (the triangular patch of grass in front of the church), have both unfortunately been lost since this picture was taken.

Esther Christian, Bride Postmistress from 1897-1910, and her daughter Esther Kinrade, Postmistress until 1963, pose outside the post office in 1909. The Bride Wesleyan Methodist Chapel, seating 180 and erected by Robert Corkill of Ramsey in 1877 at a cost of £741, is in the background.

This study, posed outside Midwood's studio on the South Promenade, shows Johnny Craine on the stiff-cart belonging to Ballavarkish (Mark's farm), Bride. For over one hundred years Ballavarkish has been owned and farmed by the Quark family, originally from Andreas, and the name Quark can be made out on the side of the cart. The farm passed to a descendant of the family, David Luce, Ballawannell, in the 1980s.

Daniel Joughin Senior poses on the Cronk Bane (White Hill), Bride trap, c1908. The Joughin family have owned the farm since before 1600 and the eldest son in most generations has borne the name Daniel. Mark Henry Joughin, who was drowned on the Ellan Vannin in 1909, was a member of the family.

Point of Ayre lighthouse was built in 1818 by Robert Stevenson, grandfather of Robert Louis Stevenson, and stands 106 feet high. A lower lighthouse was erected near the original one in 1890, as material deposited from the erosion of the west coast meant the original beacon was no longer sufficiently near the water's edge. This part of the coast can be very dangerous, with the tides from each side of the Island meeting to form what is known locally as the Streuss or 'contention'.

The *Fenella* leaving Ramsey Harbour.

SOME FURTHER READING

The following books deal exclusively with Ramsey and the north of the island, but there are hundreds of works dealing with the Isle of Man that cover the area to some extent. The out of print titles should be available in local libraries or through good second hand bookshops.

Barritt, Joan   *Ramsey, Child of NCH*, 1980

Gelling, Alan   *Play Up Ramsey; 100 Years History,*
                                          of Ramsey Football Club, 1985

Harrison, H.W.   *South Ramsey And Its Churches*, 1923

Kermode, R.D.   *Annals of Kirk Christ Lezayre*, 1954

Kewin, Arthur   *Kirk Bride, Its Church And Parish*

Lomas, W.H.   *Parish Church of St. Olave*, 1981

Looney, J.C.   *Reminiscences of Old Ramsey, 1891*, 1905

Ramsey Town Commissioners   *Official Guide To Ramsey*, 1905 to date

Quayle, G.E.   *Legends of A Lifetime*, 1973

Radcliffe, William and Constance   *A History of Kirk Maughold*, 1979

Radcliffe, William and Constance   *Maughold And Ramsey Place Names*, 1978

Radcliffe, William and Constance   *Kirk Bride: A Miscellany*, 1982

Radcliffe, William and Constance   *St. Paul's, South Ramsey*, 1972

Radcliffe, Constance   *Ramsey 1600-1800*, 1986

Radcliffe, Constance   *Shining by the Sea*, 1989

Radcliffe, Constance   *The Big Snow of February 1895*, 1995

Seybold, W.N.   *The Ramsey Lifeboats, 1829-1991*, 1991

Williamson, L.E.   *A Short History of Ramsey Grammar School*, 1972

Although sadly never collected together in book form, the journalism over many years of the late Sydney Boulton forms an invaluable source of reference on the history of Ramsey.